P9-APG-090

"Here we meet the sages of old through these rarely heard female voices. The power of the awakened mind comes through these poems, resonating through time and space like a clear bell. This book will stop you in your tracks."

—Kittisaro and Thanissara, authors of *Listening to the Heart: A Contemplative Journey to Engaged Buddhism* and cofounders of Dharmagiri, South Africa

"Curl up with a cup of tea and let these poems speak to your heart. Then let your heart follow the path to freedom."

—Bhikshuni Thubten Chodron, author of *Buddhism for Beginners* and founder of Sravasti Abbey

"Warmhearted, authentic, uplifting, and moving. This gem of a book deeply affirms why and how we keep practicing through periods of darkness and light. Weingast has adapted these poems from the original Pali with wisdom, love, and poetic intelligence based on years of practice and insight."

—Nirbhay N. Singh, editor of the journal *Mindfulness*

"This collection of poems shifts our perspective and opens doors where before there were only walls. The metaphors are simple—a bowl, falling snow, a warm blanket, a knock at the door—and the unfoldings inside us profound. Though the voices are distinctly female, the revelations, inspirations, and encouragements are wholly human. This is a book to share. As one poem suggests, some rivers we must cross together."

— Rosemerry Wahtola Trommer, author of *Naked for Tea*, *Even Now*, and *The Miracle Already Happening*

"This powerful, beautifully translated collection of poems gives us direct insight into the lives of bhikkhunis at the time of the Buddha and their very human struggles and breakthroughs on the Path to Nibbana. A treasure trove of inspiration that will uplift the hearts of sincere seekers everywhere, reminding us that we, too, have the potential to be truly free."

— Bhikkhuni Canda, founder of Anukampa Bhikkhuni Project, UK

"An amazing rebirth of the *Therigatha*—deeply rooted in ancient times, yet also refreshing and meaningful to contemporary hearts. A new way of looking again."

— Bhikkhuni Santacitta, cofounder of Aloka Vihara Forest Monastery, California

"The voices of the first bhikkhunis in this contemporary rendering of the *Therigatha* are vulnerable, tenacious, and ardent. Through the poems the women are felt and alive; they viscerally impact me. Because of the recent revival of full ordination for women, there are not yet many elders within modern burgeoning bhikkhuni communities. The intimacy, intensity, and insightfulness of these voices help to fill the gap."

—Bhikkhuni Ahimsa

"A glorious portrait of the human condition through the spiritual, intellectual, and cultural experiences of women in Dhamma. The first Buddhist nuns saw value and relevance in the mundane, highlighting subtleties that men have historically ignored in the panorama of spirituality. The inherent wisdom of the female reality combined with natural storytelling instincts is elemental, intense, and sensitively direct."

—Bhante Buddharakkhita, author of *Planting Dhamma Seeds: The Emergence of Buddhism in Africa* and founding abbot of Uganda Buddhist Center, Entebbe

"This inspiration of the *Therigatha* carries the sweetness of freedom, the angst of pain and suffering, the exhilaration of humor, the depth and pith of profound wisdom, and the delicate tender care of pure love. These women remain powerful archetypes for our path—past, present, and future."

—Larry Yang, cofounder of East Bay Meditation Center and author of *Awakening Together: The Spiritual Practice of Inclusivity and Community*

"Though thousands of years old, the voices of these awakened Buddhist women can be heard with freshness and clarity in this new interpretation of the *Therigatha*. These brief poems boldly proclaim the path to liberation, inspiring us to rededicate ourselves to our own paths and practices."

—Mushim Patricia Ikeda, Buddhist teacher and author of "Daylighting the Feminine in American Buddhism" in *Innovative Buddhist Women: Swimming against the Stream*

"I felt as though I was walking the path of practice right beside these women. Their struggles and their release from struggle were palpable and resonant. These poems ring with authenticity and timelessness. I love this collection."

— Susan O'Brien, Dharma teacher at Insight Meditation Society

"This book is a treasure trove of women's voices expressing the path to liberation and liberation itself. It brings to life the earliest expressions of this tradition through the feminine perspective."

— Brian Lesage, guiding teacher at Flagstaff Insight Meditation Community

The First Free Women

Poems of the
Early Buddhist Nuns

Matty Weingast

FOREWORD BY
Bhikkhuni Anandabodhi

SHAMBHALA
Boulder
2020

Shambhala Publications, Inc.
4720 Walnut Street
Boulder, Colorado 80301
www.shambhala.com

9 8 7 6 5 4 3

Printed in the United States of America

♾ This edition is printed on acid-free paper that meets the
American National Standards Institute z39.48 Standard.
♻ Shambhala Publications makes every effort to print on recycled paper.
For more information please visit www.shambhala.com.

Shambhala Publications is distributed worldwide by
Penguin Random House, Inc., and its subsidiaries.

Designed by Kate Huber-Parker

Library of Congress Cataloging-in-Publication Data
Names: Weingast, Matty, translator. | Anandabodhi, Bhikkhuni,
author of foreword.
Title: The first free women: poems of the early Buddhist nuns /
Matty Weingast [translator], foreword by Bhikkhuni Anandabodhi.
Description: First edition. | Boulder: Shambhala Publications, 2020. |
Includes indexes.
Identifiers: LCCN 2019013712 | ISBN 9781611807769 (paperback)
Subjects: LCSH: Buddhist poetry—Translations into English. |
Pali Poetry—Translations into English.
Classification: LCC BQ1452.E5 W45 2020 | DDC 294.3/8232—dc23
LC record available at https://lccn.loc.gov/2019013712

CONTENTS

Foreword

These poems you hold in your hands are like jewels to me. They call us to remember our greatest potential—our potential to be free.

They first arrived in my life at the end of a month-long retreat. Matty, who was also sitting that retreat, mentioned to me with some trepidation that he'd been working on a translation of the *Therigatha* (*Verses of the Elder Nuns*). I had a feeling from the few words he shared that this was going to be a translation unlike any I had read before, so I asked to take a look.

As I was reading those still-unfinished poems, chills ran through me over and over again. Some of the poems touched my heart, others shook me up, and some revealed teachings that I hadn't seen so clearly before.

I had been waiting a long time for a rendition of the *Therigatha* that would speak directly to my heart. There are several English translations, but most have been done by scholars who have remained in a formal relationship with these poems composed by enlightened women 2,600 years ago. While these academic translations of the *Therigatha* may be literally accurate, and with some effort the inspiring teaching can be found, for me they miss the quality of transmission and so remain as words spoken long ago, now dusty and dry.

Reading through this new rendition, feeling the visceral response, and experiencing the sense of clarity and connection that came through, I realized that Matty had taken these poems far beyond what I had hoped for.

At times it has been a struggle to make my way as a Buddhist nun. Both the support and the modeling that elders can give has been missed. Much of our history and the legacy we receive through the Pali canon can be pretty tough. Nuns are often framed as being a problem, simply by fulfilling our aspiration to give ourselves wholly to the path of awakening. It's challenging when a purehearted intention is met with opposition within the very community to which you belong, just because of your physical form.

There were times when the challenges and misunderstandings felt insurmountable. For a while, all of the nuns in the community where I lived were being publicly admonished for not understanding the teachings, for being overly identified with our gender, and for not being sufficiently grateful. I would sit and feel the impact of that while staying strongly connected with my clear intention to practice for awakening.

Staying present with the dissonance between my inner experience and those outer challenges became like an alchemical process. There was a sharpening and strengthening of spiritual qualities under this intense fire. For a time, I was able to use that experience as a tool for transformation. But at some point, one has to align one's inner truth with the outer environment—and move on.

Over the past thirty years, a worldwide revival of the Theravada *bhikkhuni* order has been evolving. Slowly but surely, the opportunity for women to take full ordination is opening up again. It is a natural reemergence of what has been kept down for so long—a birthright that can now, at last, be reclaimed.

Scholars are gradually unearthing a less prejudiced history of these courageous women. Scholarly work and literal translations are essential, but we also need transmissions of the heart that can speak to us directly in this contemporary time. *The First Free Women* provides a link to the founders and lineage holders of this order. These renditions carry the voices of our enlightened foremothers, women from all walks of life who found the path to Freedom. I can hear them. I can feel them. They have come alive.

Living as a nun for the past twenty-five years, I have felt that I should present to the world what's good, what's inspiring, what's beautiful. In order to do that, I sometimes have to push away or put on the shelf parts that are not so beautiful and inspiring. I feel as though my spiritual practice has gone to a whole other level since becoming involved with these poems—both because of the joy they've given me and because they invite a wholeness that I had never quite allowed before.

There are so many different kinds of women speaking here—princesses and sex workers, young lovers and wives in arranged marriages, women who were quick to gain insight and women who had to struggle for years, until one day it finally opened.

Somehow, they all found the Path. They all realized awakening.

For me, these poems have been an invitation to bring light to the hidden corners and the broken parts, to the confused parts and the angry parts, to all the parts that have been pushed aside. Because it's only when we bring everything onto the Path that the Path can truly transform us. Most likely it will be messy at times. It won't always look the way we think it should look. But if we have the courage to shine light into those forsaken places and welcome whatever we find there, as Rohini ~ Wandering Star says in her poem,

> then
> you will know
> the true welcome
> that is the very essence
> of the Path.

May these poems bring you joy, insight, inspiration, and guidance along the way, just as they have done for me.

Bhikkhuni Anandabodhi

A BRIEF NOTE

At the end of the monthlong February retreat where I told Bhikkhuni Anandabodhi that I had been working with the *Therigatha*, she and I sat down and went through each poem together. Many she read aloud, pausing now and then to point out the parts that felt true and the parts that still needed work. Her encouragement, as well as her deeply intuitive sense of what each poem wanted to say, not only gave a new burst of energy to the process—it gave direction.

Later that summer, I flew out to Aloka Vihara Forest Monastery to continue working on the poems with her. The two weeks that I had planned on staying turned into four months. During that time, all of the nuns and guests contributed to the shape and the feel of these poems in one way or another.

Many of the poems in this book closely resemble the originals, with shifts here and there of varying degrees. Others are more like variations on a classic tune. Though these are not literal translations, even in the freest renderings I don't hear my voice. I hear Uppalavanna, Khema, Mahapajapati, Anopama, Patachara, Siha, Dhammadinna, Isidasi. In all cases I worked with the original Pali texts and consulted all available English translations.

For the ease of readers unfamiliar with Pali, all names have been spelled phonetically. For those interested in a more traditional translation, I recommend those by Susan Murcott, Charles Hallisey, and K. R. Norman.

On first glance, the *Therigatha* appears to be a collection of largely straightforward, self-contained structures. But closer inspection reveals any number of secret rooms and hidden passageways, some of which keep going deeper and deeper the further you go. I'm certain that I never reached the bottom. And I hope that others continue to work with these poems and find depths and worlds in them that I could not.

Not surprisingly, the question that has come up most often is about my being a man working with the verses of the first Buddhist nuns. Many have asked how the project began, what my intentions were, and why I didn't instead work with the parallel collection of poems by the first Buddhist monks. In the end, perhaps the best I can say is that I never intended to translate anything, but that the voices of these women spoke to me and deeply moved me.

I'm incredibly grateful to have been a part of this book. The time I've spent with these poems has been the happiest of my life. They've changed how I relate to the path, and they've given me glimpses of its true scope. I truly hope that these poems touch your heart just as they have touched mine. And I even hope that these poems will change your life, just as they have changed my life.

This book is dedicated to the courageous women who began the *sangha* of Buddhist nuns, as well as to all women of all traditions who continue to put on robes, in one form or another, and walk the path to awakening.

The path must be for everybody.

Don't we all want to be free?

Matty Weingast
Aloka Vihara Forest Monastery
Placerville, California

Introduction

The *Therigatha* (*Verses of the Elder Nuns*) is one of the sacred texts of early Buddhism and the world's oldest collection of women's literature. It consists of seventy-three poems composed by some of the first Buddhist nuns—women of all ages, backgrounds, and temperaments who traveled widely varying paths.

Each poem bears the author's name as its title.

Here you'll find the incomparably beautiful.
The incomparably sad.
Those born into abject poverty.
And those born into limitless wealth.
The tired wives of arranged marriages.
And the desperately in love.
Young women who sell their bodies.
Daughters left orphaned or abandoned.
Grandmothers who spend a lifetime caring for others.
Mothers who watch their children die—and wonder how they can possibly go on.
The warriors.
The sages.
The earth mothers.

Those who refuse to do as they're told.
Those who refuse to remain silent.
Those who refuse to give up.

Their voices are all here.

Though these poems differ in subject and tone, they are all ultimately triumphant because they are all pointing to the true possibility of awakening that is available to all of us. These women were doing much more than creating beautiful poetry—they were changing the world. Shaving their heads and putting on robes was not simply a sign of spiritual dedication. It was an act of revolution.

Women who put on robes today continue to face inequalities almost everywhere they go. Buddhist nuns don't receive the same level of respect or support as monks. Full ordination for women has yet to be widely recognized as legitimate, and in some places it is even illegal.

This book requires no prior knowledge of Buddhism or meditation.

Come inside.

Make yourself at home.

THE POEMS

Anyatara ~ Anonymous

Rest, my heart,
wrapped in these
simple robes
you sewed yourself.

Like a pot of herbs
left cooking overnight,
that which was boiling
has boiled away.

That which was on fire
has all turned to ash.

Mutta ~ Free

One morning after begging for my food—
looking down at one more meal
I hadn't worked for,
hadn't paid for,
hadn't earned.

A life of debts I could never repay
pushing in on all sides
like the weight of the sea.

I blinked,
and a
tear
fell into
my bowl.

Would it always feel like this?

Just as the moon rises up
from the bottom of the sea,
a handful of rice lifted itself
from the bottom of my bowl.

And my heart rose with it.

I wish I could tell you
how it tasted—

that first bite of food
as a free woman.

Punna ~ Full

Fill yourself
with
the Dharma.

When you
are as
full
as the
full
moon—
burst open.

Make the dark night shine.

Tissa ~ The Third

Why stay here
in your little
dungeon?

If you really want
to be free,
make
every
thought
a thought of freedom.

Break your chains.
Tear down the walls.

Then walk the world a free woman.

Another Tissa

Find your true home on the Path.

Find the Path right here—
in the center
of your
own heart.

If you keep
searching in the past
and searching
in the future,
you will
search
and
search.

But your searching will never end.

Dhira ~ Self-Reliant

Look closely, my heart.

See how all things
arise and pass away—

even that
which is turning
the shapes on this page
into the sounds
and thoughts
you are
right now
silently speaking
to yourself.

When you no longer need
to read the signs
to find your way,
you'll know for yourself
that books and maps
can only get you so far.

There is a direct path.

Vira ~ Hero

Truly strong
among those
who think themselves
strong.

Truly unafraid
among those
who hide their
fear.

A hero
among those
who talk of heroes.

Don't be fooled by outward signs—
lifting heavy things
or picking fights with weaker opponents
and running headfirst into battle.

A real hero
walks the Path
to its end.

Then shows others the way.

MITTA ~ FRIEND

Full of trust you left home,
and soon learned to walk the Path—
making yourself a friend to everyone
and making everyone a friend.

When the whole world is your friend,
fear will find no place to call home.

And when you make the mind your friend,
you'll know what trust
really means.

Listen.

I have followed this Path of friendship to
    its end.
And I can say with absolute certainty—

it will lead you home.

Bhadra ~ Lucky

You always considered
yourself lucky
because things seemed
to work out
the way you wanted.

Now luck has a different meaning.

Lucky to be walking a Path
that finds peace
in the arising
and passing
away
of
each
present
moment.

Regardless
of how things
work out,
or don't.

Upasama ~ Calm

How do
you cross
the flood?

You cross
calmly—
one step
at a time,
feeling
for stones.

How do
you cross
the flood,
my heart?

You cross
calmly—
one step
at a time,
or not at all.

Another Mutta ~ Free

So this is what it feels like—
to be free.

Forever free
from playing the mortar
to my crooked husband's
crooked little pestle.

Enough.

For my mother.
For my daughter.
And for all the daughters
I might have had.

The cycle ends here.

Dhammadinna ~ She Who Has Given Herself to the Dharma

For so long,
I thought only
of the river's end.

Then one morning,
I set my paddle down
to watch the sun rise
over the eastern hills—

only to find
myself floating
somehow
gently upstream.

I promise.
It was not what I had expected.

Visakha ~ Many Branches

You say you're too busy.

That
there's
never
enough
time.

Take care of
whatever
you have
to take care of.

Then sit.

Be honest.

Do you
really think
you're going
to live
forever?

Sumana ~ Flowering Jasmine

Walk through
the mind
all day
and
all night.

When you find
each thought
ending
right
where
it began—

here your circling ends.

Uttara ~ North

Life had always been hot sweaty work.

First I learned
to control my hands,
then my mouth,
then my mind.

As things slowed,
I sank down,
down,
down—
to the bottom
of the heart's sea.

There I dug out the root of all craving—
and swam back to the surface.

The water had grown cool.
And outside, everything had grown cool.

As though
the heart
had traveled
north.

Grandma Sumana

After
all those years
looking after others,
this old heart
has finally
learned
to look
after
itself.

Each act of kindness
a stitch in this warm blanket
that now covers me
while I sleep.

Dhamma ~ Dharma

Another day
walking in circles
with an empty bowl.

Leaning on my staff
in the middle of the road,
my whole body shaking with hunger,
what little strength
I had left—
left me.

As I was
falling
to
the
ground,
I saw.

I was the spoonful of rice.

And this
whole world—
the bowl.

You can't miss, even if you try.

Sangha ~ Community

When I left the only home I'd ever known,
I thought I'd left everything behind.

But I was still carrying
all the years
of running
back and forth
and around in circles
after this or that.

Just sitting still,
those circles
have broken apart
and been carried away
by this simple wind
blowing in
and out.

All your old thoughts
like snow
falling
on
warm
ground.

Just sit back and watch.

Abhirupananda ~ Delighting in Beauty

Haven't you spent enough time
comparing your hair
and your clothes
and your face
to the hair
and the faces
and the clothes
of those around you?

See the body for what it is.

Real beauty is in
the clear open light
of the nonjudgmental heart.

Jenta ~ Conqueror

I was forever getting lost,
until one day the Buddha told me:

To walk this Path,
you will need seven friends—
mindfulness, curiosity,
courage, joy,
calm, stillness,
and perspective.

For many years, these friends and I have
    traveled together.

Sometimes wandering in circles.
Sometimes taking the long way around.

There were days when I thought I couldn't
    go on.
There were days when I thought I was
    finally beaten.

It's scary to give all of yourself to just one
    thing.
What if you don't make it?

Oh, my heart.
You don't have to go it alone.

Train yourself
to train
just
a little
more gently.

Sumangala's Mother

Free.

Finally free
from having to stroke
my husband's little umbrella
until it stands up straight.

His releases came quickly—
and with lots of grunting.

Mine has taken
a little longer—
and came with
the sound
of straight bamboo
being cleanly sliced
into two even pieces.

I now know for myself
where true release
comes from,
and where it leads.

A seat at the foot of any tree.

ADDHAKASI ~
THE WEALTH OF KASI

A night with me
used to cost more
than all the land
in Kasi.

But through all
the pricing and haggling,
I somehow lost interest
in being talked about
like a field of wheat.

Unlike any crop,
I have ripened
here in the shade
of these gentle trees.

A field for no farmer.
A land that has paid for itself.

Chitta ~ Heart

Somehow I kept climbing—
though tired,
hungry,
and weak.

Old, too.

At the top of the mountain,
I spread my outer robe on a rock to dry,
set down my staff and bowl,
took a deep breath,
and looked around.

It was windy up there.

As I was leaning back
against a large gray rock,
the darkness I had carried
up and down
a million mountains—

slipped off my shoulders
and swept itself away
on the wind.

Mettika ~ Kindness

I know my older sister passed this way.

At the top of the mountain,
I spread my outer robe
where perhaps
she once spread hers.

I set down my bowl—
and there was her staff.

The twin of my own.

Using both staffs,
I lowered myself down
and leaned back
against a large
gray rock.

I let go of the staffs—
and my hands were empty.

The mountain went on holding me.

Then it let me go.

My staff I also now leave behind.
Just in case you're ever passing this way.

Another Mitta ~ Friend

My mother always told me,

Be good—
and you'll get
everything
you ever
wanted.

Now I eat once a day
and wear only
a shaved head
and double robe.

It took some strength.
It took some courage to try
and see for myself.

The younger me would never have believed.

But these days I'm good
without having to wonder
whether anyone
is watching—
or not.

Abhaya's Mother

I once spent a week in bed with a bad fever.

My
little body
stank
from
head
to
foot.

Of course,
I never noticed
the smell
until after my fever
had broken.

Not that
this little story
necessarily
has anything
to do
with you.

Abhaya ~ Fearless

This body you carry around
is like a small child—
always wanting something.

Over the years,
body and mind have gotten
a little tangled up,
haven't they?

When one is hungry, the other eats.
When one is sad, the other cries.

Look closely.

Is there
a narrow valley
where one
ends—

and the other
begins?

Sama ~ Song

Like a dog
forever
getting ready
to sit,
all day
and
all night
I circled
my cushion.

These days,
body and mind
sit together
like old friends.

Since we aren't getting anywhere,
they eventually decided,
why not have a seat
and try to relax?

There are many paths.

Another Sama

After twenty-five years on the Path,
I'd experienced almost everything—
except peace.

When I was young,
my mother told me
that I would find true happiness
only in marriage.

Remembering her words all those years
     later,
something in me began to tremble.

I gave myself to the trembling—
and it showed me
all the pain
this little heart
had ever known.

And how countless lives of searching
had brought me
at last
to the present moment,
which I happily married.

Can you imagine?

We've been
living together
ever since,
without
a single
argument.

UTTAMA ~ GREAT WOMAN

For years I couldn't sleep.

Most nights I'd throw off the covers
and take long runs through the dark.

Nothing helped.

My sisters.

When sleepless nights come
to tear you into little pieces,

rise to meet the day
as a tree rises to meet the axe—
as a scalp bows to meet the blade—
as sparks from a dying fire
reach out to meet the darkness—
as all of our bones
someday fall softly down
to meet earth.

When you stand,
send your roots down between the stones.

When you walk,
walk like a skeleton walking to its grave.

When you lie down,
lie down like a blown-out candle
being put back in a drawer.

When you sit,
sit very
very
still.

My sisters, sit like you are dead already.

How could this world possibly
give you what you're looking for
when it's so busy
falling apart—
just
like
you?

Look closely.
Don't move until you see it.

Another Uttama

The entire Path,
and all you will ever need
to walk it,
you will find inside.

So the Buddha taught me.

Once I took a closer look,
all the running around
started to seem a little silly.

Things changed so quickly—
by the time I got anywhere,
I'd be someone else.

You are your mother.
You are your daughter.

One
moment
gives birth
to the
next.

What we do is who we become.

Dantika ~ The Elephant

While walking along the river
after a long day meditating on Vulture Peak,
I watched an elephant splashing its way
out of the water and up the bank.

Hello, my friend, a man waiting there said,
scratching the elephant behind its ear.
Did you have a good bath?

The elephant stretched out its leg,
the man climbed up,
and the two rode off like that—
together.

Seeing what had once been so wild
now a friend and companion to this
    good man,
I took a seat under the nearest tree
and reached out a gentle hand
to my own mind.

Truly, I thought, *this is why
I came to the woods.*

Ubbiri ~ The Earth

How many days and nights
did I wander the woods
calling your name?

Jiva, my daughter!

Jiva, my heart!

Late one night,
finally exhausted,
I fell to the ground.

Oh, my heart, I heard a voice say,
*84,000 daughters all named Jiva
have died and been buried
here in this boundless cemetery
you call a world.*

For which of these Jivas are you mourning?

Lying there on the ground,
I shared my grief with those 84,000 mothers.

And they shared their grief with me.

Somehow I found myself healed—
not of grief,
but of the immeasurable loneliness
that attends grief.

My sisters.
Those of you who have known the deepest
    loss.

As you cry out in the wilderness,
just make sure
you stop
every so often
to listen for a voice calling back.

Sukka ~ The Star

It wasn't so long ago
that all the men in town
knew my name.

Now that I wear a shaved head and double robe,
they don't pay any attention.
They just lie around drinking wine all day.

Why tie yourself to a bottle?

When the next watering hole is far ahead
and the last watering hole is far behind,
I could teach you how to drink
what falls from the sky.

Look at me.

Even on the darkest night,
I could show you
where to find
enough
light
to make
your way
back home.

Sela ~ The Rock

Long after the front gate swung closed
    behind me,
I could still hear them:

Why talk so much about death?
Find a husband to share your bed.
Bring children into the world
to leave behind after you're gone.

But ever since I invited my own death into
    bed with me,
I no longer feel lonely or afraid of the dark.

What do we really bring into the world?
What do we leave behind?

A gate swings closed—
then opens.

Where does it come from?
Where does it all go?

Soma ~ Happiness

He said:
How could a woman,
who knows no more than how to cook,
clean, and make babies,
possibly reach the further shore—
on the way to which so many good men
have drowned or turned back?

I said:
The mind is neither male nor female.

When directed towards the arising
and passing away
of all things,
it easily penetrates
this mass of darkness.

Be serious.

What's a few inches of meat
compared to the immeasurable reaches
of the liberated mind?

Bhadda Kapilani ~ Red Hair

After our wedding,
my husband and I put on robes together
and soon went our separate ways.

Not exactly what most would call a
    honeymoon.

Is that what love looks like?

Maybe—
when you see what love is
and what it isn't.

Marriage is hard.
The good times come and go.

True love doesn't throw a curtain
over the whole world
and imprison whoever it cares about the most
on an empty stage.

When the mind is free,
it's free of expecting
more than is reasonable
from any one person.

Another Anyatara ~
Anonymous

I was young when I left home.
And for years I rambled around.
My practice—sitting, walking, and hoping.

At first everything was new.
I didn't notice my skin drying up
or my hair turning gray.

Then one morning, there I was—
an old woman.

Where had I gotten in all those years on the
    Path?

That night I slept out in a field,
and it rained.
I felt like I belonged there—
miserable and alone in the mud.

In the morning,
I went to the nearest monastery
and threw myself down.

A nun took me in and taught me.
This body, this mind, this world.
Where they come from, where they go.
What they are, what they are not.

That night I went out to sit in the field,
and it rained.
I felt like I belonged there—
every drop of water telling me I was home.

Don't worry, my sisters.

When the road reaches its end,
you'll know it.

Vimala ~ The Virgin

My mother taught me how to sell my youth
for money and some sense of power—
just as her mother had taught her.

At our front door,
I answered the calls of passing men
with well-rehearsed lines,
laughing and lightly running a finger
along my neck and breasts.

A hunter with a baited trap.

Now I spend my days
sitting at the foot of this tree,
wearing only a shaved head
and double robe.

The legs of this naked mind
spread wide open—
ready to welcome whatever comes.

Siha ~ Lioness

People used to say
that I was so beautiful
it hurt to look at me—
like the sun.

The sun lights the whole world,
but it isn't free.
It lives its life on a leash.

I lost weight and grew pale.
My sister said I looked like a dead person.

When I finally put on robes,
my family was almost relieved.
Maybe it would help.

For seven years I wandered.
I got really good at being sad.

Late one afternoon,
I took a rope and went to the woods.

The sun was setting.

I could feel the rough fibers
against my neck
as I put my head inside.

That's when I saw—
it was just one more leash.

What goes on can come off.

SUNDARINANDA ~ JOY OF BEAUTY

One morning,
after another long night,
I was squatting on the toilet
watching it all come out.

For the first time I saw my body—
not just how it looks,
but what it does—
turning what is dear
into what is waste.

I got up and started walking.

As the sun was setting,
I passed a graveyard.

You, my sisters beneath the leaves.
As I am, so you once were.
As you are, so will I become.

There I slept.
And there I stayed—
examining this mass of flesh and bones,
contemplating the many masses of flesh and
    bones
gently rotting just beneath the ground.

Then one morning I saw—
what goes in must come out.
Not just the body.
But the mind.

What will you bring into the world,
other than what gets washed
down the toilet?

Nanduttara ~ Greatest Joy

I spent most of my teenage years
running from one bed
to another.

Any sign of warmth would do.

Each worked for a while,
until they got possessive
or mean
or boring—
or I did.

Then I got new friends,
shaved my head,
and started eating once a day.

During the long lonely nights that followed,
I would remember all the nice warm baths,
all the late nights and long mornings
waking up next to beautiful warm bodies.

One night,
shivering on the ground,
I started to cry.

It's not fair.
No matter what I do,
the other thing
always looks better.

Listen, my heart.
I know how exhausting it all gets.

Don't give up—
until you're ready
to give up
for real.

Mittakali ~
Friend of the Dark

I was always smart.

If the Path was good,
I figured it would make me
even smarter.

One night while meditating,
I watched my thoughts
piling themselves up
all around me.

My mind built a house
out of all those thoughts—
then filled that house.

Soon it was a whole city.
A whole world.

Oh, my beautiful, beautiful thoughts.
Who will look after you after I'm gone?

I swear I could weep.
I could weep for all of you.

My sisters.
Do you really want to be free?

Are you ready to leave behind
all your precious little houses—
and make your home everywhere?

It's not as hard as you might think.

First stand up.
Then walk out the door.

Sakula ~ From a Good Home

I once gave all of myself
to being the perfect wife and mother.

Then I heard the teachings of the Buddha.

I saw the arising and passing away of what
    was wife
and said goodbye to my husband.
I saw the arising and passing away of what
    was mother
and said goodbye to my children.

What was left I gave to the Path.

Oh, my sisters.
You never had to be perfect.

If there is something in these teachings
calling out to you,
it's because something in you
is calling out to these teachings.

The Path will take you
whenever you're ready—
just as you are.

Sona ~ The Tree

I brought ten sons into the world.
I thought that would have been enough.

But when my body could no longer
    conceive,
I lost heart.

Giving birth and raising children was all I
    knew.

Then a nun told me
how beings come into the world
based on countless causes and conditions.

I stayed with her—
and learned to raise a mind
that didn't conceive.

Yes, my sisters.
The years do go by.

Soon all the little pieces
that make up
this body
will go on to make up
other bodies.

See this for yourself.
Then ask me why I shaved my head.

Bhadda Kundalakesa ~ Curly Hair

I used to walk everywhere
wearing only a robe,
a shaved head,
and the dust of the road.

It was all great fun—
but I was still mistaking
the essential for the inessential,
and the inessential for the essential.

Please. I know it's a mouthful.
But can you tell one from the other?
If so, how?

Here at the end,
part of me still wants to go back
and kiss every inch
of every road
I ever walked.

But it's enough
just to say thank you—
and goodbye.

PATACHARA ~ WANDERING ROBE

Farmers turn up the soil, plant seeds,
    and wait.

All by itself,
water pours down from the sky
and turns earth into food.

After all these years
sleeping on the ground,
waking before dawn,
and begging for every meal—
where's my harvest?

Late one evening,
I was washing my feet
after another long day
of sitting and walking.

The water
poured
over
my feet
and onto
the ground.

I let my mind go,
and it flowed downhill with the water—
towards my little hut.

I went inside,
sat on the bed,
and lowered the wick of the lamp.

All by itself,
the flame
went
out.

Patachara's Thirty Nuns

Farmers take grain from the earth
and branches from the trees.
They crack open one with the other
and take what's left to feed their families.

You are all like unripe grain.
Take time to grow.

Then leave the ground behind
and let your husks be stripped away.

I promise. Less is more.

So Patachara told us.

So we sat on the ground like unripe grain.

We gave ourselves to the Path.
And the Path broke us apart.

What we feared most
is now seen for what it is.

True peace.
Freedom.

All that broke apart
was the darkness
we had for so long
been calling our whole world.

Chanda ~ The Moon

Do you remember when disease came to
    your village?
Of your family, you were the only one to
    survive.

You were just a girl.

For years you begged for your food.
Then a nun took you in.

You told her your story,
and she held you while you wept.
Then she told you her story,
and you wept with her.

Her name was Patachara.

You went everywhere she went—
and soon left behind
all that she had left behind.

When you were young,
you learned what it was
to be truly alone.

Now you know for yourself.

This freedom is something
altogether different than that.

The Five Hundred

Yes.
Your daughter.

By some road she came into this world,
not because you asked her.
By some road she left this world,
not because you told her.

In between her coming and going,
she passed some time here with all of us.

Oh, the places she's been.

Next time she might be a lion
or a god
or a slave
or someone's mother—
yours.

Then it could be your turn to die young,
and her turn to chase after you.

If you really want to cry for somebody,
why not cry for yourself?

Why not cry for all of us—
who are just passing through?

Fall
on your
knees
and weep.

Get it all out.

Now get up.
You've got work to do.

Vasetthi ~ From Vasettha

When a child dies, everyone grieves.
But a mother's grief is different.
Not more real or more important.
Just different.

I can talk about it like this now.
Back then I just wandered from place to
    place.

I don't know if I ate.
I don't know if I slept.

From the bottom of that darkness,
I heard a voice.

It was just a whisper,
so I leaned towards it—
and became
a bucket
pulled slowly up
from the bottom of a well.

In the same way,
I called out to my grief
and drew it towards me.

I held my grief and gently rocked it.

Shhh, I said.
There, there.
There, there.

People sometimes ask,

Wasn't it painful?
Weren't you afraid?

Yes, it was painful.
So is giving birth.

Oh, my heart,
you mustn't fear
the pain.

Khema ~ House of Peace

He said:
When a bow rubs against the strings
of a well-tuned violin,
music flows through all the heavens
and brings life to all the worlds.

Come, Khema.
Be my little viola.
Make me your bow.

When a symphony is over,
I told him,
there's nothing left
but the applause
and some sweeping up.

After the tune you mean to play,
I would carry the encore
for nine long months—
and it wouldn't end there.

This is the song your parents played
as they watched the stars circling high
    overhead.

This is the song their parents played
as they tended their fires deep in the dark
    forest.

It is an old, old song.
But listen closely.

Far from human voices
there are songs of freedom
sung only by the wind
in the leaves.

Sujata ~
Born at the Right Time

The day began just like any other.
We dressed, ate breakfast, and went to the park.

As we were passing the Anjana Woods,
I remember someone saying,

Let's go see the monastery.

We pushed open the door—
and there he was.

How did I know?
It was the eyes.

I sat down,
and the Buddha
taught me the Dharma.

You there.
Be ready.

Does today feel
just like
any other day?

Anopama ~ Beyond Compare

Growing up, my sisters and I had gold coins
    for toys.

When there's that much money around,
being beautiful isn't such a big deal.

Somehow we all were.

All my suitors started off talking about beauty—
and ended up talking about money.

One prince told my father,

Give me your daughter.
And I will give you eight times her weight in gold.

That night my father kept passing me the
    mashed potatoes
and ordered extra dessert for the entire table.

For some reason I was remembering those
    gold coins
and how we sometimes put them in our
    mouths.
The taste of gold is something you never forget.

When my thoughts drifted back to the table,
my father was staring at my half-eaten
    pudding.
I could see in his eyes that he was doing the
    math.

That night I cut off my hair,
climbed out the window,
and walked away.

I knew it would be a long journey.
At least I was starting on a full stomach.

That was many years ago.

Looking now at these old hands,
I can't help thinking
the prince's offer was a little silly.

Any day now,
the crows and dogs
will get all this—
for nothing.

Know your price, my sisters.
Don't accept less.

Mahapajapati ~
Protector of Children

I know you all.

I have been your mother,
your son,
your father,
your daughter.

You see me now in my final role—
kindly grandmother.

It's a fine part to go out on.

You might have heard
how it all began—
when my sister died
and I took her newborn son
to raise as my own.

People still ask,

Did you know then what he would become?

What can I say?
What mother doesn't see a Buddha in her child?

He was such a quiet boy.

The first time he reached for me.
The first time I held him while he slept.
How could I not know?

To care for all children
without exception
as though each
will someday
be the one
to show
us all
the
way
home.

This is the Path.

Gutta ~ Guardian

Going forth is no game.
We leave whole lives behind—
not just people and possessions.

All your wants.

All your fears.

All the little rituals
that get you through the day
and tuck you in at night.

Only see that all these pretty wooden pieces
aren't you—
and don't belong to you.

They belong to the game.

I know it's comforting to count up all the
    squares,
run your fingers along the edge of the board,
and plan out all your moves ahead of time.

The world beyond the table only seems
    dark—
like empty space.

It's okay to be afraid.

Vijaya ~ Victor

When everyone else was meditating,
I'd be outside circling the hall.

Finally I went to confess.
I'm hopeless, I said.

The elder nun smiled.

Just keep going, she said.
Nothing stays in orbit forever.

If this circling is all you have,
why not make this circling your home?

I did as she told me,
and went on circling the hall.

If you find yourself partly in
and partly out—
if you find yourself drawn to this Path
and also drawing away—
I can assure you,
you're in good company.

Just keep going.

Sometimes the most direct path isn't a
straight line.

ANOTHER UTTARA ~
CROSSED OVER

I asked Patachara,

What is the Path?

Patachara said,

Just see all thoughts, words, and actions
arising all by themselves—
not from some imaginary point within.

I only partly understood.
But I took a seat.

As the sun was setting,
I saw the endless line
of one thing leading to another
that had brought me
to the cushion
that night.

As the moon was coming up,
I saw the arising
and passing away
of all things
in every direction.

As dawn was breaking,
wisdom rose in the east—
and set fire to the long dark night.

But don't take my word for it.
Set fire to the darkness within.

I promise.
It's like nothing you've ever seen.

Chala ~ The First Sister

What will be the last voice you hear—
right before you cut the chains of the world
    forever?

Will it be someone
who loved you
and cared for you?

And did you abandon them?
Did you break their heart?

It's not too late, they'll say.
You can still come back home.

In between
the passing away
of one voice
and the arising of another—
is the Path.

Freedom.

UPACHALA ~ THE SECOND SISTER

I left home soon after my sister.
She found a cave, I a community.
Typical middle sister—
always the social one.

The voice inside my head always used to ask,

Why do I have to be the middle sister?
Never first. Never last.
When is it my turn to feel special?

These are our stories.

First.
Second.
Third.

I thought the Path would make me feel
    special.

But instead it sang
such deep rich tones
that the voice inside my head
just couldn't help
but sing along.

If you're going to tell yourself a story,
why not tell yourself a story of freedom?

Sisupachala ~ The Third Sister

First one sister left.
Then the other.
Then it was my turn.

While meditating late one night,
I entered a deep stillness.

A figure emerged from the background.

It could be anyone.

Maybe someone you once loved.
Or maybe someone you still love.

Whoever it is, they'll promise.
They'll threaten.
They'll say whatever will hurt the most.

Here in the stillness, you'll break.
Or you won't.

Many of you have already been practicing
for some time.

Sooner or later you have to get in there
and see what you're made of.

This isn't about how green the grass is—
or how blue the sky.

This is about freedom.

Vaddha's Mother ~
A Mother's Mother

My mother put on robes when I was just a child.
Can you imagine?

I was angry that she had shaved her head
and made herself so ugly.

Years later, she came back.

She was still wearing robes.
Her head was still shaved.
But somehow I no longer found her ugly.

She called me to her and said,

Just remember, my daughter.
There is only the Path.

Then she left again.

From that day on,
I could feel the Path growing inside me—
sometimes kicking and punching,
sometimes quietly napping,
sometimes gently humming to itself.

When I felt like I was going to explode,
my mother was there.

It's coming, she said.
Just relax.
Let go.

Say it however you want.

You carry the Path.
The Path carries you.

In the end—
when it's your time—
the final push
will come
from a strength
you never imagined
you had.

Kisagotami ~ Skinny Gotami

A child dead.
And a mad search for a magic seed.

It's a story as old as dust.

Brave up, my sisters.

The day will come
when you run
from house
to house.

People will meet you at the door,
look you in the eye,
and they won't let you in.

I'm sorry, they'll say.
But we can't help you.

Listen.

When everyone you love is gone,
when everything you have
has been taken away,
you'll find the Path
waiting
underneath
every rock
on the
road.

These are the words of Kisagotami.

Uppalavanna ~ Blue Lotus

I hated my father.

And I hated my mother
for making him my father.

I left home to get away from him—
and then found him everywhere I went.

But I trained hard.

I learned to make
my hands
glow red with fire.

And I handled the darkness with a chain.

I swore—
no one
would ever
hurt me
again.

Then one night,
while meditating in the woods,
I was grabbed from behind.

This sal tree is in full bloom,
the man said.
And here lying beneath,
I find a sal flower
with a lovely shaved head.

Tell me, my little flower.
Aren't you afraid?

I turned around.
He looked just like my father.

It would have taken so little,
a flick of a finger,
to make him
burn.

I looked into his eyes
and saw the billion lifetimes
that he and I
had been running around
this same circle
together.

Then I walked
all the way down
to the darkest parts
of my own mind—
and stood in front of
the blazing roar
as countless
lifetimes
of fear
and revenge
threw themselves
into the furnace.

Burn with me, my sisters.

And when you're ready,
come up from that dark place
where you've gone
to be alone
forever.

The Path leads directly through
these vast worlds of fear and hate.

We have all wounded and been wounded.
We have all been made to feel weak.

Yes.
There is great strength in the darkness.

Yes.
The mind can be used as a knife—
or a chain.

Yes.
Your whole world
is burning
itself
to the
ground.

Ask the lizard how long this has been
    going on.
Ask the sunflower and her million seeds.

The mind is more powerful than you can
    possibly imagine.

Ask yourself what
you are really
prepared
to give up
in order to be free.

Punnika the Slave

In the early morning,
well before dawn,
I would go down to the river.

It was my job to carry water
up the hill
to my master's house.

Of course.
We all want to be free.

But what good is freedom,
when your sisters remain slaves?

I used to imagine an old man down there by
    the river.
I used to imagine what I would say to him.

What does it mean—
to own another human being?

What does it mean—
to feel your own skin,
to touch it,
and know you are not free?

We all have bodies.
My sisters, I don't have to tell you.

But where did I get this body?
Who made me a slave?

The old man and me—
standing here,
watching the river.

Waiting.
But for what?

Over the years,
this round
heart
has been
pounded flat.

Sometimes it doesn't feel safe—
to feel anything at all.

Don't give up, my sisters.

Whatever you have to say,
now is the time to say it out loud.

All our dreams of the past.
All our dreams of what will be.

Come.
Reach out your hand.

Some rivers we must cross together.

AMBAPALI ~
GUARDIAN OF THE MANGO FOREST

All the hairs on my body
used to buzz like black bees
whenever I was touched.

Now they're like the hairs on dead bark.

This is the story
of how one thing
changes into another.

I used to wear flowers in my hair.

Hours after I walked by,
you could take a deep breath
and know I had passed that way.

These days I still leave some scent behind.
But most would rather I didn't.

My hair used to flow down like a black silk
    river.
My body was a port for all travelers.
But those waters have long since dried up,
and ships plan their routes around other stops.

Things change.
They just do.

My eyes were once deep dark pools.
Men got lost in them.
That's how I remember it now, anyway.

It's hard to know what's true
and what to believe in,
when true beauty
so quickly turns
into this.

How did such a perfect nose
turn into this funny little potato?
And what's the point of earlobes?
Are they just there to hang trinkets from?

You out there. Do you have teeth?
Are they white or yellow?
Straight or crooked?

Sooner or later, they're all coming out.
That's just how it is.

These hands once danced and played
like two sisters on a stage.
Now they sit around all day
like peppers drying and cracking in the sun.

How could we have let it matter so much—
knowing that someday it would all come to
    this?

You were beautiful once.
Or maybe you're still beautiful.

Tell me.
Where will you go when it all falls apart?

But maybe you're not ready just yet
to take to the open road all alone.

For now,
just see the body
as a house you're renting
for a short time.

Make the heart your home.

Please.

Stop telling yourself
you have all the time in the world
to change your life.

Rohini ~ Wandering Star

You don't become the cloth
just because you put on robes.

You don't turn into empty space
just because you carry a bowl.

The sun doesn't bow down.
Trees don't throw flowers at your feet.
Birds don't start answering when you call.

The Path will hold even the biggest mistakes.
The Path will make room for even your
    deepest regrets.

But you don't become
the cloth of the robe
overnight.

It can begin very quietly.
Something you barely even notice.

Like the touch of water on your skin,
like a knife in a drawer,
like the next five minutes—
unless they're your last.

The Path isn't a line on a map.
It's a great shining world.
Enter wherever you like.

You might get thrown back once or twice,
but if you push through
the outer layers—
oh, my sisters,
then
you will know
the true welcome
that is the very essence
of the Path.

Chapa ~ The Archer

Love is like all things.

One night it's knocking at your front door.
The next morning it's waving you goodbye.

My sisters.

The thing that breaks
and leaves sharp edges
that cut you from the inside—
that's not the heart.

That's the house you built
out of all the pretty things
other people told you,
and the strange promise
that what is felt today
will still be felt tomorrow.

But such houses are built to fall apart.

And when they do,
the heart must take to the open road
and leave the past behind.

At first I thought I couldn't live without him.

Then I realized
there were certain things
that for a long time
I had been unwilling
to admit—
even to myself.

Look me in the eye, my sister.

You are more than your laughter
and your sighs.

You are more than your rage
and your tears.

You are much more than your body.

Sundari ~ Beauty

We've all heard
the stories
about
young
women
who walk
across the world
to find their fathers.

And the endless tests and trials—
to prove who they really are.

But these stories often don't end happily.

What do you really have to prove?
And to whom?

Through the beginningless turnings of birth
    and death,
you have had countless fathers.

But know this, my child.
You were born of the Dharma.

Look.

See
how
you are
changing
even now—
as the Buddha,
like a rising sun,
races across
the world
to claim
you
as his
own
true
daughter.

Subha the Goldsmith's Daughter

They all told me the same thing,

There's only one way to be truly safe.
Get as much as you can—
and hold on tight.

We don't take greed seriously enough.
I grew up in a house made of gold,
so I ought to know.

You see what it does to people.
Slowly.
Over time.

It changes them.
It takes over.

You find yourself saying,

I'll learn to be generous.
I'll give it all away.

But first
I just need
a little
bit
more.

Stop lying to yourself.
See a clenched fist for what it is.

Not tomorrow.
Not in twenty years.

Now.

I am Subha the goldsmith's daughter.
Eating whatever is offered.
Sleeping wherever I can.

This is what freedom looks like—
not a bucket of coins buried out back.

Just like you,
I spent a long time
going back and forth.

But eventually I had to stand up
and say it out loud:

I will not be owned.

Subha of the Jivakamba Woods

One night I was walking
through the Jivakamba Woods,
when a man appeared
on the path in front of me.

I could just make him out in the moonlight.

Those shapeless robes
can hide your body,
the man said,
but they can't hide your eyes—
like two moons rising
over the Jivakamba Woods.

The man walked towards me
until we were face to face.

He winked.
And smiled.

I could have cried out.

I could have fought.

I could have run.

Instead I closed one eye
and held up a thumb,
like a painter measuring her subject.

The man's smile widened,
then slowly changed,
as I brought
my thumb
towards my face,
dug the thumb into my socket,
and pulled out the eye.

Yes. There was blood.

Here, I said,
taking the man's hand,
gently opening it,
and placing the eye inside.

The man looked at me as though lost.
Then he looked down at the eye.

My sisters.

When we aim too closely—
sometimes we miss.

Close your eyes.
See things as they really are.

One night in Jivakamba,
a man with the worst of intentions
saw through all illusions
and found his freedom.

Why shouldn't you?

Isidasi ~ Attended by the Wise

Isidasi and Bodhi were sitting together
after their morning meal
in a shady corner of the Pataliputta Forest.

Bodhi said to Isidasi,

How did it happen, my sister—
that you came to leave home?

And so Isidasi told Bodhi her story:

My father gave me everything I asked for.
When I came of age, he gave me to a
    wealthy merchant.

I cared for my husband
as a mother would care for
her only son.

And like a spoiled child,
he constantly complained
and humiliated me in front of others.

When his parents asked him why,
my husband only said,

She is in every way the perfect wife.
Still, I can no longer live in the same house
as Isidasi.

They took me back to my father's house—
and left me there.

Soon my father gave me to another rich
    merchant,
but with only half the dowry.

I lived in Number Two's house
and served him as a slave would serve her
    master.
And in turn he treated me
as a master would treat a slave.

After a month or so, he too sent me back.

One morning a wanderer came to our door.
He and my father got to talking,
and my father said to him,

Good man, put aside your robes and bowl.
Stay here with us—
and take my daughter as your wife.

The wanderer and I lived together as
   husband and wife
for two whole weeks.

Then one morning he said to my father,

Good sir, give me back my robes and bowl.
Once again I will take to the open road.

Your daughter is, in all ways, the ideal
   companion.
Still, I can no longer live in the same house
as Isidasi.

That night I couldn't sleep.
Something inside was pulling and twisting.

In the morning I gave myself to the Path—
and the Path took me away.

I remember those first weeks and months.

At night I was often cold.
During the day I was often hungry.
And I was lonely all the time.

While meditating late one night,
I saw far, far back—
back to before I was ever Isidasi—
back to when I was the daughter of a
    poor man
who was always in debt.

I saw the afternoon when a rich merchant
came to collect on a debt—
and my father gave him me instead.

When I came of age,
the merchant's son took me for his own.

And even though I served him as best I
    knew how,
after a couple of weeks, he started to
    complain.

And somehow I wasn't surprised by what
    came next.

Listen, my heart.

When they send you away,
make sure you wave goodbye
with both hands.

One river flows towards you.
Another away.

In the end,
you will be the one
to carry yourself
home.

Sumedha ~ Great Wisdom

I was wearing a new white dress
on the morning I first heard the Dharma.

Something was calling,
but I couldn't quite make it out.

I started spending more
and more time
alone in my room.

One morning over breakfast,
my mother asked me what was going on—
so I told her.

The Buddha's Path isn't easy to follow,
my mother said,
especially for someone accustomed to getting
whatever she wants.

Marry the good King Anikadatta.
Enjoy all the things young ladies enjoy—
dressing up,
being waited on,
and going to expensive parties—
like weddings.

"Today you want to dress this body up
and sell it at a wedding," I told her.
"But soon enough they'll be selling it to the
    graveyard
for nothing.

We are cows chasing the axe.
We are soft flesh chasing the cobra's fangs.
We are dry straw chasing the torch.
We are lovers chasing our own reflections.

Mother.
We are walking food.

The vultures circle,
we lie down,
and the feast begins."

My parents watched
as I took a long sharp knife
and cut off my long black hair.

Just then King Anikadatta walked in.

He looked at me—
blade in one hand,
a couple feet of hair in the other.

Then he smiled.

With your hair cut short, Sumedha,
you look even more beautiful.

Soon all the women in our kingdom
will be cutting their hair
just like yours.

Come, my love.
The whole world is chasing happiness.
You and I will be among the lucky few
who win the race.

"Good King," I said,
"If we spend our lives
running after the things of the world,
we will die
and keep right on running—

stealing the things we mean to earn,
setting fire to the things we mean to protect,
drowning the people we mean to love,
and turning into enemies those most like
    ourselves."

I threw my hair to the ground.

Anikadatta knelt down,
picked up a few strands,
and let them fall.

Then he stood and turned to my parents.

You who would have been my mother.
You who would have been my father.
Let Sumedha go.

May she find the Path.

And may she one day return—
to show us all the way home.

It's getting dark now, my sisters.

The sun's going down,
and soon we'll all be going
our separate ways.

Can we sit here together
just a little while longer,
not saying anything at all?

The Path will go on
rising and falling
like a song—
and in the end
you will find yourself
as one lost at sea
finds herself
finally washed ashore.

Listen.
Can you hear that?

The sound of the wind
in the leaves,
like a wave coming on.

Go on.

Shake up the world.

Set yourself free.

Acknowledgments

This book would not have been possible without the following people. Some contributed their feedback and ideas, others their friendship and support. Bhikkhuni Anandabodhi, Bhikkhuni Dhammadinna, Bhikkhuni Santacitta, Bhikkhuni Ahimsa, Samaneri Dhammadipa, Lorraine Weingast, Parker Huber, Lisa Bilotta, Dawn King, Laurie Phillips, Sebene Selassie, Rachel B. Glaser, John Maradik, Lila Kate Wheeler, Lorena Weingast, Nico Weingast, Ryan Weingast, Joel Weingast, Mindy Zlotnick, Josh Bartok, Shannon Anderson, Linda Furrow, Tracy Van Zandt, Carol Ennser, Meredith James, Sumedha Hannah, Susan O'Brien, Caroline Jones, Stephanie Seldin, Pam Baricklow, Breanna Locke, Nirbhay Singh, Abigail Campbell, Elizabeth Vigeon, and Aloka Vihara Forest Monastery.

Deep thanks to Liz Shaw for her care and patience.

Deep gratitude also to Susan Murcott, Anne Waldman, Caroline Rhys Davids, Ajahn Thanissaro, Charles Hallisey, K. R. Norman, and Anagarika Mahendra for their translations of the *Therigatha*.

INDEX OF POEMS BY TITLE

INDEX OF POEMS BY FIRST LINE

Note: In some cases, several lines have been included to make it easier to identify the poems.

Matty Weingast is co-editor of *Awake at the Bedside* and former editor of the *Insight Journal* at Barre Center for Buddhist Studies. With almost two decades of meditation experience, Matty completed much of the work on this book while staying at Aloka Vihara Forest Monastery in northern California.